TIME CHRONICLES

The Enigma Plot

Written by Roderick Hunt
and illustrated by Alex Brychta

Before you begin ...

Dear Reader,

Before you begin this Chronicle, you should know that Biff, Chip, Kipper and friends have become Time Runners. They are based in the Time Vault, a place that exists outside time. Their mission is to travel back in time to defeat the Virans.

Virans are dark energy in human form. Their aim is to destroy history and so bring chaos to the future.

The Time Runners have to be brave and self-reliant. They have a Zaptrap, which is a device to capture the Virans. They also have a Link, which is a bit like a mobile phone disguised as a yo-yo. The Link lets them communicate with the Time Vault. Apart from that, when on a mission, they are very much on their own!

Theodore Mortlock
Time Guardian

The Enigma Machine, 1941

During World War 2 the Nazis sent secret messages using machines called 'Enigma'. The message was typed on the machine's keyboard. Every time a key was pressed, the Enigma machine changed that letter. Messages became totally scrambled and almost impossible to decode. Unless, that is, the person who received the message also had an Enigma machine and knew the settings. If only Britain could crack the Enigma code!

Chapter 1

The Major stared at the papers on his desk and gasped. Then he spoke to the woman sitting in front of him.

"You scored 96% in our test. It's the highest score I have ever seen."

The woman's eyes met his. They were so cold and piercing, they made the Major shudder.

The woman gave an icy smile. "Yes," she said. "I like working out puzzles and I enjoy solving codes."

The Major gulped. His eyes were locked in the woman's stare. He felt a coldness creep up his body.

"I see you speak fluent German and Russian," he said.

The woman spoke softly. "I speak many other languages."

She stared coldly at the Major.

"Well, er, Miss Vinar," he went on. "You can begin at once. The work is a vital part of the war effort." The Major found it hard to speak properly. "It is, and must be, absolutely secret. Abso ... er ... secret ... lutely."

He picked up a paper. The woman gently pulled it from his hand. "Ah! The Official Secrets Act," she said.

As she signed the paper, her eyes did not leave the Major's. "You will find I am very good at my work," she said.

"Can't ... think ... cold ... so ... why ... I ... am?" the Major gasped.

"Oh, I can," hissed Miss Vinar.

Chapter 2

Neena was beating Wilf at computer tennis when the alarm went off in the Time Vault. Tyler was pressing the alarm button, on ... off ... on ... off! The call was urgent.

"It's a tricky one," Tyler said when everyone was in the control room. "I can't quite make it out."

A dark spot had appeared on the TimeWeb like a black hole.

"It looks as if the Virans are on to something big," said Neena.

"It's high up on the web," said Kipper, "so it can't be that long ago."

Tyler keyed the Matrix. Then he peered at the globe that glowed beside it. "Somewhere in England in 1941," he said. "Look, it's a big house near a railway line. I don't get it."

"Well, 1941 was near the beginning of World War Two," said Biff. "So what are the Virans up to?"

"Who's going on this one?" asked Chip.

"I think Wilma," urged Neena. "But let her choose who goes with her."

Tyler tapped the portal key on the Matrix, and at once, a doorway appeared next to the TimeWeb. Wilma, Nadim and Kipper stepped into it. "Good luck," called Wilf as Tyler tapped the 'send' key on the Matrix.

Chapter 3

The three of them arrived together.

They were in a corridor that smelled of polish, disinfectant and sour milk.

From behind a door they could hear children chanting.

"Four nines are thirty six. Five nines are forty five ..."

"It's a school," said Wilma. "These are classroom doors."

Suddenly, a bell rang and children began to rush out of the classrooms. It was home time.

"Don't run!" shouted a man's voice.

One boy lagged behind. As he ran out, a girl tripped him up. A few children began to chant, "Evacuees, dirty knees. You've got nits and lice and fleas."

"We've got to stop this," said Wilma. "Come on!" She ran to the group of children. "Leave him alone," she yelled.

The children looked surprised.

"Who are you?" one asked. "We ain't never seen you before."

"Never mind who we are," said Wilma. "Clear off! You're just a load of bullies."

The children ran off. As Kipper pulled the boy to his feet, he saw he had been crying.

The boy told them that he had been evacuated in June 1940 with all the children at his school.

"It's safer in the country, in case of bombs. But I miss my Mum. She's still in London. I worry about her."

DOWNLOAD FROM TYLER

In World War II, kids living in big towns went to live in the country. In 1940 100,000 were evacuated! Imagine it!

"I was evacuated to Bedford," the boy went on, "but the people I live with, Mr and Mrs King, moved to Bletchley. They both got jobs here so I came with them. I'm the only evacuee in the school."

Nadim took his Link from his pocket. They needed help from Tyler back in the Time Vault. "Tyler," he whispered. "Why are we in a school?"

"Dunno," Tyler's voice crackled over the Link. "But listen! Get to a big house called Bletchley Park. Loads of people work there. They intercept Nazi messages in code and try to decipher them. It's very secret and hush-hush. Guards everywhere!"

"So we just walk in, do we, and zap a Viran or two?" said Nadim, grimly.

"It won't be easy," said Tyler.

16

A car hooted impatiently outside the school gate. "That's Mr King," said the boy. "He picks me up every day. He's on the staff at Bletchley Park. He works in the grounds. So I help him until the end of his shift."

"Ah!" said Nadim. "Nice one! I think we may have found the way to get into Bletchley Park."

Chapter 4

Mr King was glad that Peter had found some friends. Peter was a shy boy who missed his mother. It was not easy for a nine-year-old to be sent away from home to live with strangers. No wonder he cried so often, and sometimes wet his bed.

"What a terrible thing the war is!" sighed Mr King. "It's a battle everyone has to fight, not just soldiers."

When they got to Bletchley Park, Mr King left the four children to play football and got on with his work.

"Don't go near the house," he warned.

Peter punted the heavy, leather football at Kipper.

"Ouch!" yelled Kipper. He had tried to head the leather football. "Don't you have a plastic ball?" he complained.

"What's plastic?" asked Peter.

Wilma was listening to her Link. "Tyler's got something," she said. "The Nazis have machines, called Enigma, that scramble messages into code before they are sent out. Then they use machines to unscramble them at the other end. Here, at Bletchley, they get hold of the coded messages. It takes weeks to break the codes even though they have copied the Enigma machines."

"But if they have the same machines here, why is it so hard?" asked Nadim.

"The Enigma machines have millions of settings," said Wilma. "The Nazis change them all the time, so the codes are never the same."

"What if they've found a way to break the codes more quickly?" said Nadim, excitedly. "If they knew the settings, they could crack the codes and see what the Nazis are up to."

"What if the Virans did something to stop it?" agreed Wilma. "Then our mission is to zap the Virans first, before it's too late. It won't be easy. Look."

They glanced across at the house. It was a large, rambling building with odd windows, archways and pointed gables. Next to it were rows of wooden huts.

A number of men and women had come out of the huts to sit on the grass in the sun.

"It's hard to spot any Virans among that lot," said Kipper.

One woman sat away from the others. Something about her was different.

"Hmm! Hang on," said Wilma. She ran towards the woman, dribbling the football.

"Bet you can't tackle me," she called loudly to the others. But as Wilma ran closer to the woman, she took aim and kicked the ball towards her.

The ball smacked quite hard against the woman's legs. The woman glared at Wilma with icy, blue eyes. A shadow passed over the sun. Wilma suddenly felt very cold.

"I'm ... I'm so sorry!" stuttered Wilma.

The woman stood up slowly. "Careless of you," she hissed. Then she walked off to one of the huts.

Wilma ran back to the others.

"I think I know who the Viran is," she said. "So now what are we going to do?"

"Let's wait till dark," said Nadim.

Chapter 5

"It's what we've all been hoping for," said the Major. "A Nazi submarine has been captured. On board was an Enigma machine, and a book giving us the settings."

He beamed at the others in the hut and waved his hand at a small machine. It had keys like a typewriter and three wheels with letters on. Next to it was a book of settings.

"Here they are," said the Major. "Safely delivered to Bletchley Park. Now we know the settings we can crack the codes in hours."

Suddenly, he saw Miss Vinar was staring at him. To his surprise, she handed him a drink.

"A toast," she smiled. "I've been saving it for this very moment, when we had some good news like this."

It was not like the icy Miss Vinar to be friendly. "Of course," the Major gulped. "To Enigma," he cried, holding up a chipped tea cup.

Suddenly, the lights went out with a pop. The hut was thrown into darkness. A voice shouted for an emergency generator to be switched on, but nothing happened.

Candles and torches were found. As light returned to the hut the Major's heart raced.

The machine, the settings and Miss Vinar had gone.

Chapter 6

Kipper yawned. He had been crouching in a bush for what seemed like hours, waiting and watching ...

All the huts were dark, with not a chink of light coming from any door or window. Tyler had told him it was because of the wartime blackout.

DOWNLOAD FROM TYLER

Everyone has to cover their windows and doors at night with thick, black curtains, cardboard or paint.

Until then, the moon had cast a silvery
light on the huts. But suddenly, the moon
vanished and an inky blackness came down,
as if a giant hand had covered the moon.

Kipper heard someone in the hut shouting
about a power cut. Then he saw a figure
creep out and away into the darkness.

He spoke urgently into his Link. "Wilma!
Nadim! It's her! The Viran! Coming your
way. She's carrying something."

Miss Vinar had only minutes to get away. Her plan was simple. In the darkness she just had to run to the fence where she had cut a hole the night before. Then, it was only a short dash to the railway line.

She would place the Enigma machine on the track to be smashed under a train. She would jump on the same train to get away. Then her work would be done. She had also taken the book of settings. Stealing them from the code breakers at Bletchley would unravel history. Britain would lose the War.

But what she had not expected was that two children – Nadim and Wilma – would jump into her path. One of them raised an arm as if to throw something at her.

In her surprise, she dropped the heavy Enigma machine and leapt sideways, past the children, into the darkness.

"I couldn't zap her," shouted Wilma.

As the moon came out, they saw the Viran running. "She's getting away," Nadim yelled as they raced after her.

"She slipped through the fence," panted Wilma. "Quickly! We must get closer or the Zaptrap might miss."

The whistle of a train sounded. The Viran was thinking fast. She decided to jump on the train from the bridge. As long as she had the book, her plan would succeed.

But suddenly, in the moonlight ahead of her, was a small figure. It was Peter.

Wilma gasped. What was he doing?

Peter ran towards the Viran with his arms out. The Viran stumbled, and pushed him aside, but she had been slowed down.

"Peter, run!" shouted Nadim, as he threw his Zaptrap.

The Zaptrap clicked open. It flew towards the Viran like an angry insect. The Viran burst into a shower of sparks as the Zaptrap sucked in the dark energy that once had been Miss Vinar. Peter did not see it. He was sobbing in Wilma's arms.

"I thought that woman was Mummy," sobbed Peter. Wilma held him tightly as Nadim picked up the Zaptrap and the book of settings that the Viran had dropped.

Moments later, Mr King ran up. "Peter," he gasped. "Why did you run off like that?"

Mr King said that Peter's mother had phoned to say she was coming to see him. They had gone to meet her, but she was not on the train. That was when Peter ran off.

Peter's face lit up when Mr King told him his mother had missed her train, but would be on the next one.

Nadim handed Mr King the book of settings. "Give these to Bletchley Park."

Kipper asked Tyler to get the portal ready. "Mission successful," he said.

"Who are you?" asked Mr King.

But the three of them had vanished.

Tyler's Mission Report

Location:	Date:
Bletchley Park	May 1941
Mission Status:	Viran Status:
Viran plot foiled.	Zapped!

Notes:

World War 2 must have been a scary time if you were a child. It's hard to imagine it! People were worried that children who lived in cities or towns would be in danger from bombing raids, so huge numbers of children were evacuated. That meant if there was any risk of being bombed, you were sent to live in the country with complete strangers. Children had labels tied to them, as if they were parcels. Then they went by train to towns and villages, not knowing who they would be living with or if they would be split from their brothers and sisters. Imagine Biff, Chip and Kipper being split up. They'd have hated it! And what would Floppy have done?

Sign off:..........Tyler..........................

History: downloaded!
The Code Breakers

Once World War 2 began, German U-boats attacked ships bringing food and goods to Britain by sea. A U-boat would search for the food ships. When it found them, it called up other U-boats and they all attacked together to sink the ships. This meant that it was very hard for Britain to get enough food. Britain almost lost the war because of this.

An Enigma machine

Shopping during World War 2

MINISTRY OF FOOD

RATION BOOK

OFFICIAL PAID

HOLDER'S NAME AND REGISTERED ADDRESS

Compare with your Identity Card and report any difference to your Food Office

Surname

Other Names

Address

DO NOT ALTER

ISSUED JULY 1941

If found return to

GREENWICH

FOOD OFFICE

The U-boats used Enigma machines to send messages to each other in code. Britain had to crack the code to beat the U-boats.

A secret base was set up at Bletchley Park. People worked night and day to break the U-boats' codes. They cracked the codes, but it took hundreds of hours. The problem was, the settings on the Enigma machines were always being changed, so the codes changed too. At last, in May 1941, a book was captured showing all the Enigma settings. After that, the code breakers at Bletchley were able to decipher the messages and warn the food ships about U-boat attacks.

For more information, see the Time Chronicles website:
www.oxfordprimary.co.uk/timechronicles

Glossary

codes *(page 6)* Codes are used to send secret messages. The message is replaced by other words, numbers or letters. *"... I enjoy solving codes."*

decipher *(page 16)* To work out the meaning of something that is written in code. *"They intercept Nazi messages in code and try to decipher them."*

evacuated *(page 14)* Sent away from danger. An evacuee is the person who is sent away. *... he had been evacuated in June 1940 with all the children at his school.*

generator *(page 27)* An engine which makes electricity. *A voice shouted for an emergency generator ...*

intercept *(page 16)* To get hold of something or someone as it goes from one place to another. *"They intercept Nazi messages in code and try to decipher them."*

Nazi *(page 16)* The political party that ruled Germany at the time of World War 2.

Official Secrets Act *(page 8)* Anybody who works with information about the safety of the country has to sign the Official Secrets Act promising to keep it secret. *"Ah! The Official Secrets Act," she said.*

Thesaurus: Another word for ...

decipher *(page 16)* solve, interpret, fathom out, translate.